Wind ENERGY

David and Patricia Armentrout

Rourke
Educational Media

rourkeeducationalmedia.com

www.rourkeeducationalmedia.com

PHOTO CREDITS: © auilovephoto: Header, 25; © Tulay Over: page 4; © Edyta Linek: page 5; © Pichugin Dmitry: page 7; © LoBoCo: page 8; © ansem: page 9; © Adam Kazmierski: page 10; © Govert Niewland: page 10 inset; © James Steidl: page 15; Courtesy: Library of Congress: page 15 inset; © Alberto Pomares: page 16 left; © Anthony Brown: page 16 right; © Bodil1955: page 17 top; © Alina Pavlova: page 17 bottom; © Michaela Stejskalova: page 18; © Niels Quist: page 19; © Eric Gevaert: page 20; © Drazen Valkelic: page 21; © rrocio: page 23; © Stephen Sweet: page 24; © bigredlynx: page 25; © DinaNlr4a: page 25; © Ali Azhar: page 26; © Junker: page 27; © Yobidaba: page 28, 39; © Manfred Steinback: page 29; © Alexandr Smulsky: page 30, 31; © Ian O'Hanlon: page 32, 33; © Jane Norton: page 36; © Stephen Strathdee: page 40, 41; © Iñaki Antoñana Plaza: page 42; © byllwill: page 43

Edited by Kelli Hicks

Cover design by Nicky Stratford, bdpublishing.com
Interior design by Teri Intzegian

Library of Congress Cataloging-in-Publication Data

Armentrout, David, 1962-
  Wind energy / David and Patricia Armentrout.
     p. cm.
  ISBN 978-1-60472-326-7 (hardcover)
  ISBN 978-1-61741-541-8 (softcover)
  1. Wind power--Juvenile literature. I. Armentrout, Patricia, 1960- II. Title.
  TJ820.A76 2009
  621.4'5--dc22

                    2008025138

  Printed in China, FOFO I - Production Company
    Shenzhen, Guangdong Province

Rourke
Educational Media

rourkeeducationalmedia.com

customerservice@rourkeeducationalmedia.com • PO Box 643328 Vero Beach, Florida 32964

Table of Contents

CHAPTER ONE

Wind - Energy of Motion

Have you ever flown a kite on a warm spring day? You couldn't have done it without wind. Maybe you have seen a sailboat race. It was wind power that pushed the boats across the water. Wind is the movement of air. It is energy called **kinetic energy**, or energy of motion. Kinetic energy actively does work. That means wind energy works for us!

Sunlight is kinetic energy because it actively heats and lights the Earth. **Potential energy** is stored energy that has the ability to do work later. The chemical energy your body gets from food is a form of stored energy.

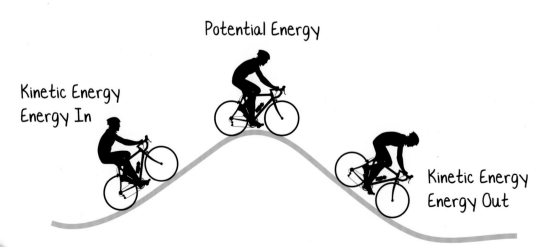

Potential Energy

Kinetic Energy
Energy In

Kinetic Energy
Energy Out

What causes wind to blow? The uneven heating of the Earth by the Sun creates wind. Earth is not smooth. It has uneven surfaces of soil, rock, water, and ice. As the Earth rotates, and the Sun shines, the various surfaces absorb solar energy (energy from the Sun) at different rates. Land and water near the equator absorb more solar energy and warm more quickly than the icy poles. Warm air naturally rises. When it does, cooler air moves in to take its place, creating currents of air, or winds.

Warm air rises.

Cooler air pushes in
to replace the warm air.

CHAPTER TWO

Energy Needs

Energy is important to everyone. In fact, no one can survive without energy. Solar energy warms our planet and helps plants grow, and we need plants for food. Wind energy also helps plants grow through **pollination**.

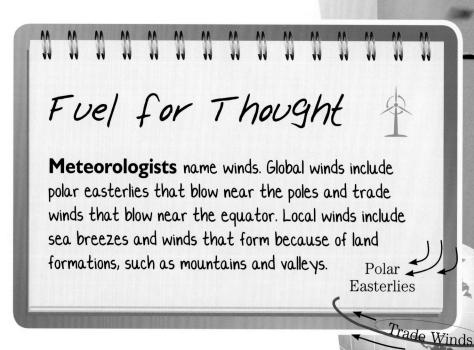

Fuel for Thought

Meteorologists name winds. Global winds include polar easterlies that blow near the poles and trade winds that blow near the equator. Local winds include sea breezes and winds that form because of land formations, such as mountains and valleys.

Polar Easterlies

Trade Winds

Polar Easterlies

Fuel for Thought

Coal is the world's primary source for electricity production. Power plants that use coal burn it to heat water and produce steam. The steam spins a **turbine**, which rotates a shaft in a **generator**. The generator converts the energy to electricity.

We need energy to produce electricity. Electricity powers everything from small appliances to huge **industrial** machines. We use electricity in our homes, schools, and businesses. Where does electricity come from? We generate it from several energy sources. According to the World Wind Energy Association (WWEA), the world currently generates 1.3 percent of its electricity usage from wind energy.

CHAPTER THREE

Global Energy Sources

Renewable Energy

SOLAR ENERGY
- Heat and light energy from the Sun
- Renews day after day as the Sun shines

WIND ENERGY
- Motion energy from the wind
- Renews day after day as the wind blows

HYDROPOWER ENERGY
- Energy from moving water
- Renews day after day in waves and flowing rivers

GEOTHERMAL ENERGY
- Heat and steam energy beneath the Earth's surface

BIOMASS ENERGY
- Plant material and animal waste used to generate energy

Fossil fuels are nonrenewable energy sources. We use them faster than they can form naturally. Wind is a renewable energy. It blows day after day. The table lists global energy sources used everyday.

Nonrenewable Energy

COAL
- Solid that takes millions of years to form
- Mined from the Earth

OIL
- Liquid that takes millions of years to form
- Pumped from the ground

NATURAL GAS
- Colorless odorless gas that takes millions of years to form
- Pumped from the ground

PROPANE GAS
- Natural gas that becomes a liquid gas at high pressure or at low temperature
- Found with natural gas and oil

NUCLEAR ENERGY
- Stored in atoms-the smallest particles of chemical elements
- Formed using uranium ore which is mined from the earth

CHAPTER FOUR

Harnessing Wind Power

People have used wind energy for thousands of years. Ancient Egyptians harnessed wind energy in sails. More than 5,000 years ago, Egyptians fitted canoe-like boats with sails and transported people and food along the Nile River. Sailing made fishing, traveling, and even fighting wars easier and more **efficient**. Sailing also affected global exploration. Christopher Columbus could not have made his voyage to the New World without his sailing ships!

Sailing is an ancient practice, but people find new ways to use old technology. One company is experimenting with kites, instead of sails, to harness wind for seagoing vessels. The kites, called skysails, look like giant parachutes. They use wind energy to tow or pull watercraft through the water. The kites are fitted to yachts, fishing boats, and cargo ships. Crews fly the skysails, adjusting their height to find the strongest winds. Skysails do not replace watercraft engines, but can reduce their need for fossil fuels.

Wind power isn't just for work, though. Creative minds have invented many ways to use wind energy for play. Kitesurfing is one example. Huge sails pull kitesurfers through the water on small boards. Riders cruise at 50 miles per hour (80.4 km/h) or more. The best kitesurfers perform high-flying jumps and tricks.

Windsurfing is another water sport that uses wind energy. Windsurfing combines sailing and surfing. A windsurfing board is basically a surfboard with a sail attached. Windsurfers sail across the water like sailors, and ride the waves like surfers. In contests, they compete to see who can go the fastest or perform the craziest stunts.

If you think sailing is strictly a water sport, then you have never heard of land sailing. Land yachts are land sailing vehicles. They are like boats with wheels. Land sailing is primarily a racing sport. Sailors race in deserts, on beaches, or in dry lakebeds. Land yachts are fast too. Some go nearly 70 miles per hour (112.6 km/h). Ice yachts are land yachts that sail on ice or snow. But, instead of rolling on wheels, they glide on runners.

Modern ships, boats, and small watercraft use sails to capture wind energy. It is easy to understand why. Wind is free, clean, and renewable. It provides power for transportation and recreation, but what else can wind energy do?

CHAPTER FIVE

Windmills

Windmills may be the first wind-driven machines. They convert wind energy to **mechanical energy**. Historians believe people from Persia (now known as Iran) first used windmills to crush grain sometime between the sixth and eighth centuries. The windmills had several vertical poles with sails. Arranged in a circle, the sails rotated in the wind above a grinding wheel. Persians used the same windmill design to pump water for crop **irrigation.**

Europeans built post windmills around the twelfth century. The post windmill design is one many people are familiar with today. Post windmill sails turn in a similar way to sails on a toy pinwheel.

The Netherlands is a country famous for its windmills. The Netherlands is a low-lying region in Europe that has flooded many times throughout history. Beginning around the thirteenth century, the Dutch built windmills to power pumps, which drained areas below sea level. They used windmills for crushing grain too. About ten thousand windmills once dotted the Netherlands landscape. Today, just over one thousand remain.

When Europeans colonized America, they brought their windmill designs with them. Windmills later played a role in America's westward expansion. As railroads moved west, so did windmill construction. The railroad used water, pumped from the ground with wind energy, for steam locomotives. Ranchers,

Fuel for Thought

Windmill production boomed in the 1900s. By 1920, American windmill makers were producing about 100,000 farm pump mills a year. Production declined after power companies installed electricity lines.

farmers, and homesteaders also used pump mills to draw water for livestock and crops. Living in the Great Plains in the 1800s would have been difficult without pump mills.

CHAPTER SIX

Wind Turbines

A wind turbine is a modern machine that converts wind energy to electrical energy. There are different types of turbines. The most common type is the horizontal-axis turbine. A modern design of this type looks like a giant airplane propeller affixed to a tower.

Fuel for Thought

Windmills convert kinetic energy to mechanical energy. Wind turbines convert kinetic energy to electricity, a potential energy, which later performs the work.

CHAPTER SEVEN

How Turbines Work

A modern wind turbine has three basic components: a rotor, a generator, and a support tower. The rotor is a system of rotating blades. The generator is a machine that converts energy to electricity. It receives kinetic energy from the blades through a shaft and gear system. The generator and other parts sit inside a housing called a **nacelle**. The tower, made of tubular steel, steel lattice, or concrete, supports the nacelle and the rotor.

Nacelle Enclosure
*contains the components
that generate electricity*

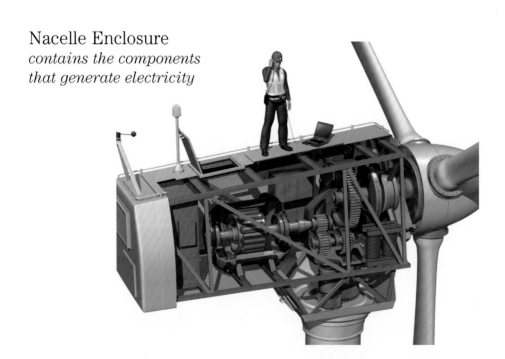

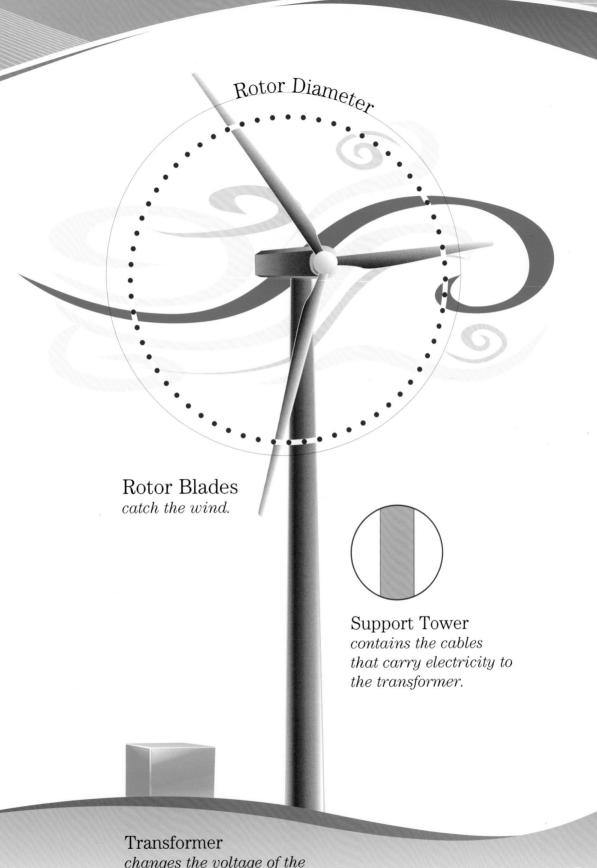

Rotor Diameter

Rotor Blades
catch the wind.

Support Tower
*contains the cables
that carry electricity to
the transformer.*

Transformer
*changes the voltage of the
electricity so that it can be transferred.*

Upwind turbines have blades that face the wind. They require a special motor and **wind vane** to keep

the blades pointed in the right direction. Downwind turbines operate facing away from the wind and do not need a special motor. In both systems, wind blows over the blades causing them to lift and rotate. The rotating blades turn the gear shaft system, which spins the generator and converts wind energy to electricity.

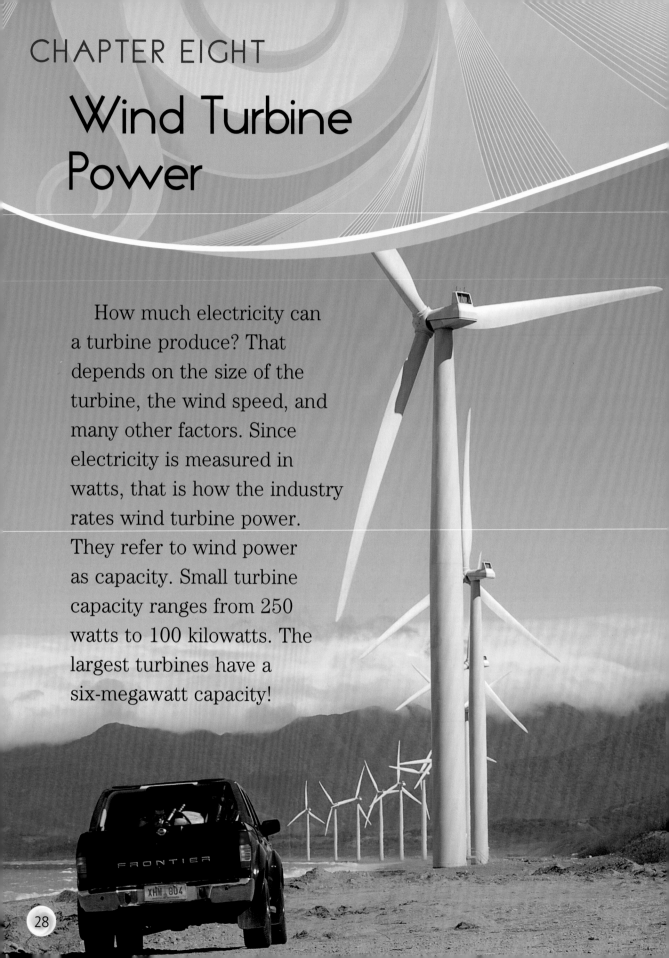

CHAPTER EIGHT

Wind Turbine Power

How much electricity can a turbine produce? That depends on the size of the turbine, the wind speed, and many other factors. Since electricity is measured in watts, that is how the industry rates wind turbine power. They refer to wind power as capacity. Small turbine capacity ranges from 250 watts to 100 kilowatts. The largest turbines have a six-megawatt capacity!

Fuel for Thought

Watt is a unit
of power used to measure
electricity flow.

Kilowatt
one thousand watts

Megawatt
one million watts

Gigawatt
one billion watts

CHAPTER NINE

Small Wind Systems

A small wind system generates electricity for individual homes, farms, and small businesses. Small wind systems need plenty of room to operate. They benefit people living in isolated areas where there is no access to an electricity **grid**. Some people install them to reduce or eliminate the electricity they get from utility companies.

Fuel for Thought

An electric fan has rotating blades just like a wind turbine, but works in the opposite way. Electricity turns the blades of a fan and generates wind. Wind turns the blades of a turbine and generates electricity.

CHAPTER TEN

Wind Farms

What happens when you group several wind turbines in one location? You create a wind farm. Wind farms generate electricity for power grids. Power grids distribute electricity to many homes and businesses. Wind farms may have a few turbines, or hundreds of them. Depending on the number of turbines and their size, a wind farm generates enough electricity for hundreds, or even thousands of homes.

CHAPTER ELEVEN

World Wind

There are thousands of wind farms in more than 70 countries. Germany has more wind farms than any other place in the world. A German company builds the world's largest turbines, and has installed several of them. The giant machines are 453 feet (138 meters) tall. The diameters of the rotors are 413 feet (126m).

The United States has been the leader in new installations for the past three years. The U. S. wind power capacity is over 16.8 gigawatts. That is enough energy to power about 4.5 million homes.

Dallas ★

Horse Hollow Wind Farm

Houston ★

Texas generates more wind energy than any other place in the U.S. It is home to the largest wind farm in the U.S., and in the world. The Horse Hollow Wind Energy Center spans 47,000 acres. It has 421 wind turbines with a capacity of 735 megawatts.

Fuel for Thought

What is the world's wind power capacity? According to the WWEA, world capacity reached 93.8 gigawatts at the end of 2007.

CHAPTER TWELVE
Advantages and Disadvantages

Wind energy has many advantages. The biggest advantage is that wind energy is green energy.. Green energy is friendly to the environment. Wind turbines do not burn fuel. Therefore, they do not release harmful **emissions** into the air.

Of course, wind turbines need wind to generate electricity. That is one of wind energy's disadvantages. Many places in the world do not have sufficient winds to support a wind farm. In addition, some people oppose new wind farms because of their size, appearance, and the impact they have on wildlife.

Conservation groups claim migratory bat and bird populations suffer, because they occasionally fly into spinning turbine rotors. Government agencies, turbine companies, and conservation groups study the flight paths of these animals before new wind farms are constructed.

WiND...

is the fastest growing energy
source worldwide.

. . . .

energy cannot supply all the power needed
in a single area.

. . . .

energy producers often receive a tax credit
from the government.

. . . .

farms are installed in a relatively short period of time,
compared to fossil fuel power plants, and they do not
pollute when they generate electricity.

. . . .

farms cover many acres of land.

...BUT

it's expensive to start a system, and not every place has enough wind to benefit from it.

. . . .

we can combine wind systems with other renewable energies such as solar energy systems, creating a hybrid system.

. . . .

tax credits expire. People need to urge the government to renew credits so companies are encouraged to install more farms.

. . . .

factories that burn fossil fuels generally produce wind turbine parts.

. . . .

energy companies lease land from farmers and ranchers. The landowners make money, crops have room to grow, and livestock have room to graze.

CHAPTER THIRTEEN

Working Together

All energy programs have advantages and disadvantages. Many people see issues differently, but if people work together, they can find responsible solutions.

Agencies like the U.S. Department of Energy, the World Wind Energy Association, and the American Wind Energy Association work hard to support growth in renewable energies. Power companies do their part too. With continued research and improved **technology**, wind energy will become more efficient and less expensive. Then, more people will be able to take advantage of this free, clean, and renewable energy, and the planet will benefit too!

CHAPTER FOURTEEN

Wind Energy Timeline

500-900 AD

The Persians develop windmills to crush grain and pump water.

Late 1100s

The English develop windmills to crush grain.

1300s

The Dutch develop windmills to drain water from low-lying areas.

1600s

The Dutch colonize New Amsterdam (now New York City) and introduce their windmill designs to the New World.

1800s

Windmills begin to dot the American Great Plains as the railroad and settlers move westward.

1888

Charles Brush builds the first electricity-generating windmill in Cleveland, Ohio. Later, General Electric buys his company.

1920s

Wind turbines generate electricity for thousands of rural areas across the Great Plains.

1941

The world's first megawatt-size wind turbine operates in Vermont.

1970s

The U.S. government and NASA work together to improve wind turbine technology.

1971

The world's first offshore wind farm operates off the coast of Denmark.

1973

The price of oil increases causing great interest in renewable energies.

1977

The United States Department of Energy forms.
Operation of the National Renewable Energy Laboratory (formally Solar Energy Research Institute) begins in Boulder, Colorado.

1980s

The U.S. government provides tax credits for the use of renewable energies.
California wind farms power 250,000 homes.

1990s

More efficient wind turbines replace early models in California.

2000s

Interest in wind energy grows as fossil fuel prices increase and their supplies decrease.

Glossary

efficient (uh-FISH-uhnt): working without wasting energy

emissions (I-MISH-uhnz): harmful chemicals released into
the air

fossil fuels (FOSS-uhl fyoo-uhlz): coal, oil, or natural gas
formed from the remains of prehistoric plants and animals

generator (JEN-uh-ray-ter): a machine that converts energy
to electricity

grid (GRID): system that transmits and distributes electricity
from power plants to customers

industrial (in-DUHSS-tree-uhl): having to do with factories
and other businesses

irrigation (IHR-uh-GAY-shun): supplying water to crops
with
a system of pipes and channels

kinetic energy (ki-NET-ik-EN-ur-jee): energy of motion

mechanical energy (muh-KAN-uh-kuhl-EN-ur-jee): energy of motion that performs work

meteorologists (MEE-tee-ur-OL-oh-jists): people who study the Earth's atmosphere

nacelle (nuh-SELL): an engine enclosure

pollination (POL-uh-NAY-shun): the transfer of plant pollen

potential energy (puh-TEN-shuhl-EN-ur-jee): energy that is possible

technology (tek-NOL-uh-jee): using science and skills to improve upon things

turbine (TUR-bine): an engine driven by air, water, steam, or gas

wind vane (WIND-VAYN): a device that rotates to show the direction of the wind

Index

Further Reading

Morris, Neil. *Wind Power*. Black Rabbit Books, 2007.
Povey, Karen. *Energy Alternatives*. Gale Group, 2007.
Spilsbury, Louise and Richard. *The Pros and Cons of Wind Power*. Rosen Publishing, 2007.

Websites to Visit

www.doe.gov/forstudentsandkids.htm
http://powerhousekids.com

About the Authors

David and Patricia Armentrout specialize in nonfiction children's books. They enjoy exploring different topics and have written about many subjects, including sports, animals, history, and people. David and Patricia love to spend their free time outdoors with their two boys and dog Max.